SUGGESTIONS FOR G

1. **THE ROOM** Discourage people from sitting [...] all need to be equally involved.

2. **HOSPITALITY** Tea or coffee on arrival ca[...] Perhaps at the end too, to encourage peop[...] might be more ambitious, taking it in turns to bring a dessert to start the evening (even in Lent, hospitality is OK!) with coffee at the end.

3. **THE START** If group members don't know each other well, some kind of 'icebreaker' might be helpful. For example, you might invite people to share something quite secular (where they grew up, holidays, hobbies, etc.). Place a time limit on this exercise.

4. **PREPARING THE GROUP** Take the group into your confidence, e.g. 'I've never done this before', or 'I've led lots of groups and each one has contained surprises'. Sharing vulnerability encourages all members to see the success of the group as their responsibility. Ask those who know that they talk easily to ration their contributions, and encourage the reticent to speak at least once or twice – however briefly. Explain that there are no 'right' answers and that among friends it is fine to say things that you are not sure about – to express half-formed ideas. However, if individuals choose to say nothing, that's all right too.

5. **THE MATERIAL** Encourage members to read each session *before* the meeting. It helps enormously if each group member has their own personal copy of this booklet (so the price is reduced either when multiple copies are ordered or if you order online). *There is no need to consider all the questions.* A lively exchange of views is what matters, so be selective. You can always spread a session over two or more meetings if you run out of time!

   For some questions you might start with a few minutes' silence to make jottings. Or you might ask members to talk in sub-groups of two or three, before sharing with the whole group.

6. **PREPARATION** Decide beforehand whether to distribute (or ask people to bring) paper, pencils, hymn books, etc. If possible, ask people in advance to read a Bible passage or lead in prayer, so that they can prepare.

7. **TIMING** Try to start on time and make sure you stick fairly closely to your stated finishing time.

8. **USING THE CD** There is no 'right' way! Some groups will play the 15-minute piece at the beginning of the session. Other groups do things differently – perhaps playing it at the end, or playing 7/8 minutes at the beginning and the rest halfway through the meeting. The track markers (on the CD and shown in the Transcript) will help you find any question put to the participants very easily, including the Closing Reflections, which you may wish to play (again) at the end of the session. Do whatever is best for you and your group.

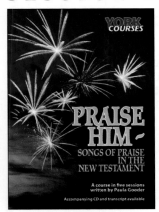

GRATITUDE

Gratitude: Ephesians 1.3-14

When one of my daughters was very small, I – as so many other parents up and down the country have done – was trying to teach her to say her 'pleases and thank yous'. She wanted a crisp. 'So what do you say?' I enquired. 'Peese,' she lisped. So far, so good. I gave it to her. 'And now what do you say?' She looked at me with that determined stare of a toddler. 'More.' Not quite the outcome I had desired!

This raises the question of why we so determinedly teach our children to say please and thank you. On the surface the answer is very straightforward: we want them to say please and thank you in order to be polite. But maybe there is another, deeper answer as well.

There is a connection between *saying* thank you and *being* grateful. As we all know, just saying the polite thing is unacceptable if it is clear the other person doesn't really mean it. Any parent trying to teach their children to say sorry has learnt this the hard way. Wringing a 'sorry' out of them, when they clearly do not mean it, is disappointing in the extreme. So when I taught my children to say 'thank you', I hoped and prayed that through learning to say 'thank you', they might also learn to feel it too.

A tumble of words

Living a life filled with gratitude is one of the markers of our Christian faith. The words of Ephesians 1.3-14 reflect a glorious example of someone who feels profoundly grateful. Gratitude simply flows out of them, word after word, phrase upon phrase, of wondering, overwhelming praise.

Ephesians 1.3-14 is one of a number of hymn or poetry-like passages in the New Testament. Perhaps they were first written as hymns or poems by the earliest Christians and later found their way into the New Testament. Or maybe these poems were composed by the New Testament letter-writers themselves. Either way, each of the passages we will be looking at throughout this course contains the most sublime poetry about Christ: who he was, and is.

The first thing to notice about this 'song' is the way the words of praise tumble out of the author. In Greek (the language of the New Testament) verses 3-14 are just one single sentence – all flowing from the first phrase:

Blessed be the God and Father of our Lord Jesus Christ, who has blessed us in Christ with every spiritual blessing in the heavenly places ...

It is almost as though the author is overwhelmed by the wonder of what he is saying. The words just spill out without any pause for breath at all. Everything in this passage is based on this first phrase: God has blessed us; so we must bless him. God has poured out glorious good things on us in Christ; the only possible response to this is ... PRAISE!

Half empty; half full?

We often talk about optimism and pessimism as though they are personality traits, and to a certain extent they are. Some people seem to find it much easier than others to look on the bright side of life. Some people's glasses are most definitely half full; whereas others seem only to see theirs as half empty. Passages like this, however, remind us that while optimism might be a personality trait, gratitude is not.

Gratitude is, if you like, a spiritual discipline. Passages like this one in Ephesians 1 remind us of the importance of rehearsing all the good things that God has done for us. It might take the form of this complex poetic passage, or it might take a much simpler form – simply spending time each day remembering what God has done for you. Gratitude is something that we can learn to do. This is what I meant when I called it a 'spiritual discipline'.

Sleeping with bread

One of the books about prayer that has had the greatest impact on me is a simple, small book called *Sleeping with Bread* (by Dennis Linn et al, 1994). It opens by telling the story of the people who worked with child survivors of the concentration camps after the Second World War. To begin with, the children were so traumatized by what had happened to them that they struggled to sleep. Until, by chance, one worker made a discovery. If the children went to bed holding a piece of bread, they could sleep – knowing that come the morning, they could be sure of having something to eat.

Developing a habit of reminding ourselves of all God has done for us and praising him for it can be the spiritual equivalent of this. If we go to bed each night holding for our *spiritual* nourishment a sense of praise for all God has done for us, then over time we will become more and more aware of what he has done – and is doing – in the world.

The more aware we are of what God has done and is doing, the more reason there will be to praise. And the more reason there is to praise, the happier we will be. Indeed, a number of recent studies have traced the direct connection between gratitude and happiness. In surveys, people who are deliberately and consciously grateful for things in their lives are regularly found to be quantifiably happier than those who are not.

Of course, happiness isn't *why* we praise God, it is merely an important by-product of that praise. We praise God because when we encounter who he really is and all he has done in the world, praise is the only adequate response. This brings us full circle back to Ephesians 1. Over and over again we are reminded of what God has done for us in Christ. Two features in particular stand out.

Welcome to the family!

The first is that *'he has destined us for adoption as his children through Jesus Christ'* (Ephesians 1.5). It is hard for us today to appreciate quite the depth of significance this phrase carried in the first century. From time to time in the ancient world, people from outside the biological family of the householder were adopted. Ancient families were widely extended, and so this was not just to give them the sense of belonging that comes with living in a household. Rather, what it meant was that the adopted person would now be able to inherit what belonged to the head of the household.

This is clearly what's meant here, because the theme of inheritance returns in verses 11-14. *In Christ, we will now inherit everything that belongs to Christ.* We have been transformed from being outsiders to the most favoured of insiders. We are no longer rootless or hopeless; we now have a firm and promised future. We are now beloved children of God, with all the rights and privileges that come with that.

I was treated and loved like his family ... Both were wonderful and active Methodists and they showed me what Christianity was really all about.

Anonymous contributor to BBC Radio 4's Listeners Say Thank you Spot

People who have faith were so lucky; you didn't want to ruin anything for them. You didn't want to plant doubt where there was none. You had to treat such individuals tenderly and hope that some of whatever they were feeling rubs off on you.

from Blue Diary *by Alice Hoffman*

Amazing Grace

The second feature we find in this passage is that God has also revealed the deep mysteries of his will to us. So we know with confidence that this world is not all that there is. God will gather up everything, both in heaven and on earth, in a perfect unity.

There is more – much more – in this wonderful passage. But these themes are enough to be going on with. A good summary of this passage seems to me to be found in verses 7-8: *'the riches of his grace that he has lavished on us.'* As Christians, we stand in the position of receiving far more than we could ever dream of. God has lavished on us the riches of his grace. He has:

- adopted us as his children
- forgiven all our sins
- revealed to us that everything in heaven and earth will be gathered up into him

To take this seriously is to put God and his Kingdom, rather than ourselves, at the centre of our lives. It is a natural human instinct to focus solely on ourselves and our loved ones. The lavish generosity of God draws us to himself in praise, just as its warm rays draw us to the sun. We no longer exist just for the benefit of ourselves and our own families; we now *'live for the praise of his glory'* (Ephesians 1.12) with all that this entails.

[For him – James K A Smith], worship is not merely expression, the upward act of the gathered people of God, or whoever. Worship is formative, where something happens to us.
Paul Bickley, Director of Political Programme for Theos

*

The word 'Eucharist' comes from the Greek word for 'Thanksgiving'. It reminds us that gratitude should be a universal Christian characteristic.

Canon John Young, author

QUESTIONS FOR GROUPS

BIBLE READING: Ephesians 1.3-14

> *Some groups will address all the questions. That's fine. Others prefer to select just a few and spend longer on each. That's fine, too. Horses for (York) Courses!*

1. **Read Psalm 95.1-2.** Think of a few occasions when you have felt genuinely grateful for something. Share some of these with each other. In your view is there a link between gratitude and happiness?

2. On track 2 of the course CD (and transcript) our participants are asked, 'Are you a "glass-half-full" or a "glass-half-empty" kind of person?' What about you? Is looking on the 'gloomy' side sometimes the truly realistic attitude? Or should we 'always look on the bright side of life'? Look back on your life and give examples.

3. **Read Psalm 4.8** and re-read the para about child survivors of Auschwitz (p.3), then consider Archbishop Justin's words on track 9 of the CD or transcript. What strategies help you 'switch off' at night? How does gratitude feature – if it does?

4. **Read 1 Thessalonians 5.16-17.** Can you think of a time when your attitude changed because you reminded yourself of all you have to be grateful for? Do you think Cicero is right? (See box on p. 2.)

5. **Read Galatians 6.2.** Is there a downside to gratitude? Can it make us over-dependent on another human being – and therefore become unhealthy?

6. **Read Philippians 4.4-7.** Is there a danger that in trying to be grateful all the time we might become insincerely cheerful and unrealistic about the difficult times of life?

7. **Read Psalm 10.1; Psalm 13; Romans 8.28** and perhaps listen to the CD participants [track 7]. If we give God the credit for everything that goes right in our lives, should we also blame him for the things that go wrong? Do you think we should ever be grumpy – or even angry – with God?

8. **Read Ephesians 1.8.** What does the phrase *'the riches of his grace which he lavished upon us'* mean to you as you go about your daily life? On track 8 Archbishop Justin says: 'Grace is my favourite word in the English language.' What is your favourite word or phrase?

9. People express their gratitude to, and praise of, God in different ways; draw up a short list of these. How do you praise him? And for what?

10. **Read Romans 12.15.** When the Church of England General Synod voted for women bishops on 14th July 2014, there was much praising and rejoicing. Yet they knew that others were hurting. In such circumstances, is it un-Christian to rejoice?

11. **Read Luke 24.45; John 6.44; Acts 16.14.** On track 5 Sr Wendy expresses compassion for those who haven't been given the privilege of believing in God. Do you agree that faith is 'God-given'? Can we make ourselves more – or less – open to the gift of faith? What does this mean for our witness to those who don't believe in God?

12. **Read Matthew 5.1-12.** (J B Phillips translates 'Blessed are' as 'How Happy are'.) Do you agree with the Dalai Lama (see box at foot of p.4)? How would you answer his 'question all human beings must try to answer'?

SESSION 2

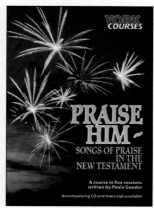

THE IMAGE OF GOD

The Image of God: Colossians 1.15-20

One of the problems of being asked to talk about our faith can be that we might have never really worked out what we want to say about it. So when someone does ask us, we fall silent, look embarrassed and change the subject.

Sometimes when talking about this, people suggest that you should imagine that you're sitting at a bus stop and see your bus coming in the distance. At that moment, imagine that someone asks you to tell them about Jesus: what would you say?

One of my favourite stories (whether true or not) about former Archbishop of Canterbury Rowan Williams is that when asked this precise question he replied: 'I would ask the person where they were going, get on the bus with them and talk with them for much longer.' The image of him getting on the bus and talking at great length with the person makes me smile and gives me comfort that I am not the only person to struggle with talking succinctly about my faith.

It may be that this problem is not reserved for believers today. Passages like the ones we're looking at in this course may be early examples of the first Christians attempting to work out how to express what they believed about Jesus, and who he was.

Colossians 1.15-20 certainly seems different from most of that letter. These verses are poetic, almost rhythmic. They repeat ideas (about Jesus being firstborn, the beginning, before all things). They repeat phrases such as 'in him' and 'through him' and 'for him'. They are both sparse in the language they use, and rich in the references they make.

All of this suggests that this 'song of praise' has been worked on extensively to hone ideas about:

- who Jesus Christ was, and
- what he has done for us

Some people suggest it might have been an early hymn sung by the first Christians; others that it was an early statement of faith. What it does seem to offer is an insight into what the earliest Christians were thinking and saying about Jesus.

Family likeness

One theme that emerges from Colossians 1.15-20 is the idea of Jesus being the image of the unseen God. Children are a good place to begin thinking about images of people. One of the uncanny things about seeing other people's children is the way in which they are the image of their parents – some more so than others, of course. Children often have features or mannerisms which somehow encapsulate their parents. In an odd way they can help us see their parents in a new light. Sometimes children can even help us understand something more about who their parents are.

Genesis 1.26-27 already has the idea of humans being made in the 'image of God'. There it says that God created us in his image, male and female. You might ask what the difference is between us being created 'in the image' of God and Jesus being 'the image' of God. The difference is subtle but important.

Being created 'in the image' of God means we have inherent characteristics that we share with God. Like a child with its parent, we have traits, mannerisms and similarities that reveal the nature of God. These traits include things like creativity, our ability to be spiritual, to be compassionate ... But again, like a child with its parent, we also have characteristics that are all our own and are most definitely not in the image of God.

A key difference

Jesus on the other hand *is* 'the image'. He is not 'in the image' of God but is God's image in its entirety. What this means is that if we want to understand who God is, then we look at Jesus. The invisible God is very hard to comprehend. But in Jesus he became visible.

In this early reflection on the nature of Jesus we discover that, actually, it is also a reflection on the nature of God. How do we know who God really is? We can discover something about him from Jesus himself. This is why the Gospel accounts of what Jesus did are so important – because they tell us not only about who Jesus is, but who God is too.

Of *course* Jesus could still the storm. God created the world out of chaos, so Jesus, too, could bring stillness in the midst of chaos. Of *course* Jesus healed people, because the God who created the world didn't suddenly stop creating and go off to do something else when he'd finished. When God encountered the need to carry on creating, he did so. Of *course* Jesus loved the poor and the outcast, for justice lies at the very heart of who God is. How could Jesus not seek out the people who needed him most?

This challenges us to look again and again at Jesus, and in doing so to learn more about the invisible God of whom Jesus is the image.

The firstborn of creation

Jesus is the image of God. But there is more. He is also the firstborn of creation (Colossians 1.15). In other words, not only does he reflect to us who God is, he reflects who we should be too. Just as we look at Jesus to discover more about God, so we also need to look to Jesus to discover more about ourselves – and the person that God is calling us to be.

This passage holds together perfectly the twin themes of:

● Jesus as God and
● Jesus as human being

Jesus is God's image and was there with God at the dawn of time – shaping creation into existence. He is also the firstborn of creation and reveals to us what God imagined being human could really be like. So Jesus stands at the centre of everything – reflecting God's true nature, as well as humanity's true calling to be who God wants us to be.

*

A popular adage often cited by Christians is 'WWJD?' or 'what would Jesus do?' The problem is that the question doesn't always deliver an easy or a comfortable answer. There was a joke that went around the internet for a while that said, 'When someone asks "what would Jesus do?" always remind them that losing your temper and throwing tables around is an option.' This helpfully reminds us that what Jesus would do is not necessarily to take an easy path. Gentle Jesus, meek and mild is not the Jesus we meet in the Gospels. The way of Jesus is a way of hard choices, a way that emerges out of a deep sense of integrity and honesty.

Holding it together

This brings us on to possibly the most important part of this entire passage: that Christ stands at the centre of everything in the world and that *'in him all things hold together'* (Colossians 1.17).

One of my favourite fridge magnets says: 'Don't tell me to relax, it's only my tension that is holding me together.' I certainly sometimes feel that way! What this passage reminds us is that we can relax in the knowledge that at the centre, not just of each one of us but of the whole world, is Christ – in whom, through whom and for whom the world was created and in whom, through whom and for whom God reconciled the world to himself. This Christ stands at the centre of all things and this Christ holds everything together. This Christ provides coherence in a fractured and wounded world.

If you were to try to describe what Colossians 1.15-20 is telling us about Christ, you would be forgiven for thinking that it fell into the category of 'God, the universe and everything'. To my slight shame, when I attempt to talk about my faith it begins and ends with *me*; with what Jesus has done for *me*. In talking about Christ as it does, this song of praise takes in the whole of the created world. The author tries to describe what a difference Jesus made – and continues to make – to the whole universe. I wonder what our faith might be like if we did the same?

Love (III) *by George Herbert (1593-1633)*

Love bade me welcome. Yet my soul drew back
    Guilty of dust and sin.
But quick-eyed Love, observing me grow slack
    From my first entrance in,
Drew nearer to me, sweetly questioning,
    If I lacked any thing.

A guest, I answered, worthy to be here:
    Love said, You shall be he.
I the unkind, ungrateful? Ah my dear,
    I cannot look on thee.
Love took my hand, and smiling did reply,
    Who made the eyes but I?

Truth Lord, but I have marred them: let my shame
    Go where it doth deserve.
And know you not, says Love, who bore the blame?
    My dear, then I will serve.
You must sit down, says Love, and taste my meat:
    So I did sit and eat.

QUESTIONS FOR GROUPS
BIBLE READING: Colossians 1.15-20

1. **Read Romans 12.12.** Sr Wendy says: 'I don't think I could have lived without the support, and the joy of faith.' [Track 11 on the course CD/transcript.] Has that been your experience – or do you struggle with faith? If you were asked to explain your faith in Jesus in the time it takes for a bus to arrive, what would you say?

2. Our participants talk about their favourite Christian poems [track 15]. Do you have a special poem or hymn – or perhaps a Bible verse? What is it that makes you love it so much?

3. **Read Genesis 1.26-27.** What do you understand by the Bible affirmation that we are 'made in the image of God'? Physical likeness/spiritual likeness/ability to think/love/create …? Which human characteristics best reflect our being made 'in the image of God'? Which characteristics least reflect this?

4. Do you know anyone who is 'the image' of their parents? Spend a bit of time reflecting on what it is that makes you think of them in that way. (See also Q. 12 below.)

5. **Read Luke 15.21-24** and John Donne's verse in the box below. Would you behave differently in your everyday life if you didn't believe that God is going to forgive whatever sins you commit?

6. **Read Colossians 1.15** and the Archbishop Michael Ramsey box on p. 7. Archbishop Justin says [track 13]: 'The way we know who God is, is by seeing Jesus. And the way we know who Jesus is, is through the scriptures.' Sr Wendy echoes this: 'God is mystery. It's 'Jesus talk' that makes sense to us humans.' In other words, we can learn a lot about who God is from what Jesus did and said. Reflect on the Gospel stories and share some examples that speak to you personally and affect the way you live.

7. **Re-read Colossians 1.15.** Jesus is not just the 'image of God'; he is also the 'firstborn of all creation' through whom God shows us what he wants us to be like.

Think about who Jesus was, and discuss what you think God imagined we could be like. How would you be different if you were to be more like this?

8. **Read Matthew 21.12-14.** 'Gentle Jesus, meek and mild' goes the hymn. Was he? Sometimes/often/always? Why do you think Jesus is so often portrayed in that way? Do you think we should ever follow Jesus' example of throwing tables around and speaking harshly?

9. **Read Colossians 1.17-20.** What do you understand by the remarkable statement that 'in him all things hold together'? Have you ever had that sense in your own life when you've felt that you've seen evidence of this? You might find Sr Wendy helpful here [track 14].

10. **Read Romans 8.28.** Ultimately, in this life, all things don't hold together. The fact of suffering is an immense challenge for every life. You might wish to listen again to track 7 from Session 1 and discuss what Sr Wendy and Archbishop Justin have to say.

11. Is there anything else that Colossians 1.15-20 tells you about Christ that you noticed while reading this passage but haven't had the chance to talk about yet?

12. *You might like to discuss the following in the light of our being made 'in the image of God'.* By introducing a minute amount of DNA from a 'third parent', offspring can be freed from the burden of an inherited illness. In your view should this be permitted? Or is this the slippery slope to 'designer babies'?

I have a sin of fear, that when I have spun
My last thread, I shall perish on the shore;
But swear by thyself, that at my death thy Son
Shall shine as he shines now, and heretofore;
And, having done that, thou hast done;
I fear no more.

from A Hymn to God the Father
by John Donne (c.1572-1631)

SESSION 3

HUMILITY

Humility: Philippians 2.5-11

People like Mother Teresa and Nelson Mandela are, rightly, widely respected and admired. All too often, however, conversations about great people end with something like, 'Of course I could never do that'. We love to feel inspired by other people but are hesitant about trying to emulate them.

The passage we explored in Session 2 and the verses we're looking at now are often called 'Christ-hymns' because they are clearly poetic and clearly about Christ. This means that we are often tempted to read them on their own – out of the context in which they are found in Colossians and Philippians (as, indeed, we are doing now!). The problem is that when we do this, we are in danger of missing the point of them entirely.

Practical faith

This is made very clear by Philippians 2.5: *'Let the same mind be in you that was in Christ Jesus, who ...'* In other words, this hymn is only partially about Christ. It is also – crucially – about us. This is not a passage that just invites us to stand around and admire Christ, to count the fine things he did and was and (having done so) to feel a warm glow inside.

This passage invites us to change, to think, and to be different as a result. It challenges us not just to admire Jesus, but to do our utmost to be as like him as we can. It reminds us that Christ is not someone just to be admired, but someone to be followed; not just someone to look up to, but someone on whom to model our lives. This 'Christ-hymn' offers us a vision of how to live in the world as Christ did.

The first verse of the description of Christ (v.6: *'though he was in the form of God, did not regard equality with God as something to be exploited'*) has caused huge debate, discussion and argument. The word that has caused so much trouble is translated by the NRSV as 'exploited'. Some translations put 'robbery'; some 'grasped'; some 'snatched'; some 'used to his own advantage'. Such varied translations tell us that translators struggle to find the right word.

All these words legitimately translate the Greek word *harpagmos* used here, but not all quite capture what Paul meant. The problem is that Jesus already had equality with God, so we need a word that implies holding on to something he already had, rather than a word that suggests reaching towards something he didn't already have (which is the difficulty with 'grasped' or 'snatched').

Out of the mouths of babes

When my children were much younger, I was reflecting on this translational problem just as we had some of my daughter's friends round to play. She was a toddler, so playing with other children was something she was still learning. When the doorbell rang and I went to answer it, I was aware that she was very busy picking up toys. When I returned to the room, she stood there with her arms full of her favourite toys and declared very firmly, 'These are mine!'

She remained there for the next few minutes, staunchly defending her favourite toys, while the other children got on playing with everything else. She very quickly realized the flaw in her plan. As I looked at her, I suddenly saw an answer to the translation problem! 'Clutched' (rather than 'grasped' or 'snatched') is the word that we need here.

The point is: they were *her* toys. They *remained* her toys, but because she clutched them to herself, not only could the other children not play with them, *she* couldn't play with them either. In a similar (though obviously quite different) way, Jesus was equal with God: he remained equal with God, but he didn't clutch it to himself. As a result, Jesus offered us a gift beyond measure. Human nature dictates that we cling on to the things we love the most, but the model of Jesus suggests that in doing so we spoil what we have, not only for others but for ourselves as well.

It's also worth noting that in not clutching equality with God to himself, Jesus didn't lose it. The end of the passage tells us that God gave him *'the name above every name'.* Having the mind of Christ in us challenges us not to clutch to ourselves the things we treasure, or which make us feel important, but to hold them gently and, if necessary, to be willing to let them go.

The suffering servant

A second Christ-like characteristic comes in the next verse: *'he emptied himself, taking the form of a slave'.* We need to be very careful when reflecting on this verse to make sure we don't end up saying things about

Christ that aren't true. For example, he did not empty himself of being God, nor of being able to act like God. We see this clearly in the Gospels.

I love Charles Wesley's hymn *And can it be*. I love it so much I have a tendency to sing it with more gusto than tune, but I must admit to mumbling a bit when I get to the line *'Emptied himself of all but love'*. It's a lovely line and what Wesley is trying to say there is, in one way, spot on. Jesus did not empty himself of love: Amen to that! The problem is that we need to be careful not to tip too far in interpreting this verse. Jesus did not empty himself of all but love. He certainly kept love, but he also kept other features too, not least his divinity.

Jesus emptied himself of prestige, status and position. That is the point of *'taking the form of a slave'* (v.7). Jesus – freely, willingly and joyfully – chose the position in society that no one in their right mind would choose. If being equal with God is at the top of the heap, then being a slave was certainly at the bottom.

What Jesus held lightly was his own importance. He emptied himself completely of all self-importance and embraced the one role in his society that no one else would choose. He went from being in complete control of everything to giving up control – even over his own life.

This passage challenges us to reflect deeply and carefully about what obeying this command might mean for each one of us. It is an important part of the Gospel message. Jesus himself made this clear: *'whoever wishes to be first among you must be slave of all'* (Mark 10.44). And Paul underlines it here. Yet Christians throughout the centuries have found this one of the hardest things to hear.

Status and high position are seductive. They always have been and they always will be. That inner draw to make ourselves look and feel more important is hard to resist. Yet time and time again Jesus, and now Paul in this passage, tells us not only to resist this but to go in the opposite direction – to seek out the least important places and roles.

The question for each one of us, if we take this passage seriously, is: how will this affect our attitudes and actions in daily life?

QUESTIONS FOR GROUPS

BIBLE READING: Philippians 2.5-11

1. **Read John 13.12-15.** Paul tells the Philippians to be humble, as Jesus was. Can you think of anyone (a friend or a famous person) who has demonstrated true Christ-like humility?

2. **Re-read Philippians 2.11.** In the early Christian centuries followers of Jesus were killed for asserting that 'Jesus Christ is Lord'. What does this phrase mean for Christians in today's world. Our participants discuss this on track 22 of the CD and transcript.

3. On track 20 of the CD David Suchet says, 'I'm not a very confident person. I may give the impression that I am, but I spend my life in self-doubt as well.' Can you relate to this? Is self-confidence always a good thing? Is lack of self-confidence always a bad thing?

4. Our participants discuss humility and self-esteem on track 20 of the CD - and come up with three different perspectives. How would you define 'humility'? Is it always an attractive quality?

5. **Read Romans 12.9-10.** 'A person who is nice to you, but rude to the waiter, is not a nice person' (Dave Barry, American writer). If we are all equal in the sight of God, is the way we treat other people more important than the way we view ourselves?

6. **Read 1 Corinthians 1.4.** Archbishop Justin, with his stress on the grace of God, suggests that we shouldn't claim credit for ourselves because our gifts come from God. Can we claim *any* credit for our own hard work and self-discipline in using these gifts, improving ourselves – and helping others?

7. **Read Matthew 5.5** and re-read the box on p. 12. Uriah Heep in Charles Dickens' *David Copperfield* is renowned for claiming to be humble but, in reality, being manipulative. What can go wrong when people pretend to be humble but aren't really? How much does what's in your heart matter?

8. **Read Matthew 11.25-30.** The command to humility implies that we are naturally confident, maybe even proud. But what about people who have low self-esteem? What message do you think that they need to hear?

9. **Read Luke 18.9-14.** Spiritual pride is one of the seven deadly sins. What do you understand by 'spiritual pride'? Is it okay for us to be proud of our grandchildren or children, or our prize-winning marrows? How does boasting fit into this?

10. **Read Philippians 2.6.** Here Paul describes Jesus as not clutching authority with God to himself. What do you *need* to hold more lightly? What would you *like* to hold more lightly? What difference might it make to your life if you were able to do so?

11. Imagine a church where everyone was able to empty themselves of all self-importance. Would it be very different from or quite similar to how your church community is now? Do you think it would be exciting or bland to belong to such a church?

12. In our celebrity culture, what is it about celebrities that people find inspiring/fascinating? How do you think those who remain 'grounded' despite their fame manage to achieve that?

SESSION 4

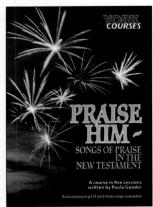

NEW BIRTH

New Birth: 1 Peter 1.3-12

The way in which correspondence begins is changing. When I was at school, we were taught very firmly the correct ways to begin and end letters. Always begin with 'Dear …' followed by title and surname 'Mrs Wilson' or 'Mr Smith' if you knew the name, or 'Sir or Madam' if you did not. Always end with 'Yours sincerely' if you did know their name and 'Yours faithfully' if you did not.

These rules apparently no longer apply and, influenced by email custom, the few letters that still come by post are changing too. I was startled to open a letter from a business the other day and find that it began, 'Hey Paula'!

Of course, how we begin letters is simply a matter of custom, and the New Testament writers had different customs from ours. Their letters begin by introducing the sender – much more logical than putting the sender's name at the end as we do. A good example is to be found in 1 Peter, which begins, *'Peter, an apostle of Jesus Christ.'* Then its recipients are identified: a group of Christians who live in middle to north-eastern Asia Minor (what we would today call Turkey). Having introduced himself and his recipients, the author plunges into a profound theological statement about God and everything he has done, beginning: *'Blessed be the God and Father of our Lord Jesus Christ!'*

Alert readers might recognize that these words are similar to the passage from Ephesians 1 that we read in the first session, and in both instances they are also followed by a description of all that God has done.

It's interesting to notice that these two openings (along with 2 Corinthians 1.3, where a similar phrase is also used) are very similar to traditional Jewish prayers. Jewish blessings often begin with words along the lines of *'Blessed are you, Lord our God, King of the Universe, who …'.*

These openings, in 1 Peter, in Ephesians and in 2 Corinthians, indicate that the earliest Christians sometimes borrowed the Jewish customs of their day when they began to talk about God. This phrase seems to help them to begin thinking about God – who he is and what he has done.

Passionate with his pen

Modern teaching techniques dictate that when you're introducing a new idea, particularly a very complicated new idea, you work up to it. You give people time to adapt, and to join you on your journey towards the idea. You introduce it gently. However the opening of 1 Peter plonks the most complex theological ideas down right at the start. This letter shows that the author does not appear to have read any of these modern teaching manuals! He explores these ideas in one long sentence. As in Ephesians 1 the words tumble out, with no pause for breath until we come to a rest in verse 12.

The whole thing is a single piece of animated, excited theology – but it has a real purpose. If we take a quick glance at the first phrase of verse 13, we can see that it explains what the author is doing in writing verses 3-12. Verse 13 of 1 Peter begins: *'Therefore prepare your minds for action …'.* In other words, what the letter says in verses 3-12 so changes our perspective on life that its readers (us included) must prepare for action. They – and we – must be ready to live out some of the ideas that have been introduced in verses 3-12.

Theology has a bad reputation for being abstract, hard to relate to and irrelevant to everyday life. We are reminded in 1 Peter 1.13 that the best theology prepares us for action. It is deeply and profoundly relevant to everything that we think and do and say. Perhaps a good litmus test for theology is how well it prepares us for living out, in our everyday lives, the truths that it reveals.

So what is the theology that's introduced in a big splurge in verses 3-12? Like the other three passages we've explored so far in this course, this passage contains so many important ideas that we can only hope to explore some of the main ones here. Two in particular stand out: new birth (verse 3) and rejoicing in the face of suffering (verse 6).

Nicodemus revisited

Verse 3 talks about God giving us a new birth. The image used here is so vivid that the translators struggle to put it into English. The NIV and the NRSV have opted for 'given us (a) new birth'. The Greek verb (*anagennaō*) is much stronger than that and literally means 'has given birth to us again'. This brings to mind Jesus' conversation with Nicodemus in John 3 about being born again. Similar words to those used by Jesus also appear in 1 Peter, but this letter is in some ways even more vivid, and ties this new birth to Jesus' resurrection. The God who raised Jesus to life from death is exactly the same God who has given birth to us again. God brings life no matter what the circumstances are.

Where God is, there true vibrant life is to be found. Indeed, life is a vital theme of this verse. God raised Jesus to life and he gives birth to us again into a living hope. 'Hope' is one of those English words that, although it is the correct translation of the Greek word (*elpis*), doesn't do justice to all it conveys. For us 'hope' is something vague, wished for but not certain. We might say 'I hope I'll see you tomorrow' – it is a good wish, but not to be relied upon.

HOPE and hope

The hope talked about by the New Testament writers is completely different. This is why the author of the letter to the Hebrews (6.19) can say: *'We have this hope, a sure and steadfast anchor of the soul'.* This is no vague general wish, but a sure and steadfast foundation that we can build our lives upon. It is referred to as a *'living hope'* in 1 Peter – a hope that is alive and also brings life. This hope raises our eyes from the lives we live now to the lives we will live with the God who is life.

This hope is connected to the harder times of life, when we are suffering various trials (1 Peter 1.6). We need to understand the word 'trials' properly. We have so over-used the phrase 'trials and tribulations' that it can now imply quite trivial things. The trials and tribulations of a day could include losing a pen and not finding a parking space!

However, the trials this letter refers to are far from trivial. The early Christians often faced persecution for their faith, and it is that great suffering the author has in mind here. And yet in verse 6, 1 Peter says that they rejoice even if they are suffering. This is a common New Testament theme and can easily be misunderstood.

There can be a tendency among Christians to be overly cheery about everything, and in doing so to appear profoundly uncaring. I have lost count of the times people have told me to cheer up because God loves me. I cannot stress strongly enough that this is *not* what is meant here.

What is meant is that as Christians we are to hold on to the long view. Suffering – physical, mental or emotional – can shrink your world so that all you see is the pain you have now. As Christians, the reason we can rejoice is because we know that 'now' is not all there is. It does not diminish or trivialize our present pain, but it fixes our eyes on a different horizon: a horizon marked by a living hope (verse 3) and the knowledge that we are ultimately protected by the power of God (verse 5).

At this point we can begin to see why this theology is so important. It gives the original recipients of 1 Peter – and us – something to cling on to in the storms of life. It doesn't belittle what we are going through, but gives us a foundation to return to, time and time again.

When my children were very young someone said to me that I should always remember the phrase 'this too will pass'. It was enormously helpful, and got me through various sleepless nights and other difficulties. What 1 Peter offers is something even more helpful than the assurance that this will pass. It offers a vision of the God of life in whom we can have absolute confidence. A better phrase for us all might be: *'God has given us a new birth into a living hope'* (1 Peter 1.3).

QUESTIONS FOR GROUPS

BIBLE READING: 1 Peter 1.3-12

1. **Ephesians 1.3** and **1 Peter 1.3** use language from a Jewish prayer. On tracks 25-27 of the CD our participants talk about their own prayer life. Does your experience echo theirs? How and when do you pray? Do set words help you – or perhaps bore you?

2. Is prayer something you find easy or hard? What do you pray for? Talk about a time when you have found prayer easiest and a time when you have found it hardest. At those times, what was it that made it easy/hard. (If the answer is you always find it hard, don't worry – you aren't alone!)

3. **Read Luke 6.12-13.** Do you/could you/will you set aside a few minutes each day or each week for prayer? Sr Wendy prays for several hours each day. How long do/would you like to spend in prayer? What, if anything, prevents you from doing so?

4. **Read Philippians 1.3-11.** How do you pray? Mainly for other people? Or do you focus on praise and thanksgiving? Or confession and contrition? Might the acronym ACTS (Adoration; Confession; Thanksgiving; Supplication) help you broaden your prayers? Share ideas within your group for broadening the scope of your prayers.

5. **Read James 5.13-16.** Can you point to a time when a specific prayer was answered in a specific way? We're told that our prayers are always answered – just not always in the way that we hope. Is this a 'cop-out'? How hard is this to hear when you are praying for someone who is unwell?

6. Theology (which means 'the study of God') should prepare us for action. Do you agree that, 'It is deeply and profoundly relevant to everything that we think and do and say.' (p. 17.) Can you give three statements about God which

help you day by day e.g. The Lord is my shepherd; Jesus is alive …

7. **Read John 3.3-5** and **1 Peter 1.3** which talk of God giving us a 'new birth'. Some people understand this to refer to a dramatic spiritual experience. Have you ever had an experience like this? Can we make a radical new start without a dramatic spiritual experience? Our CD participants [track 28] might help as you discuss this.

8. **Read 1 Corinthians 2.9.** What do the words 'living hope' mean to you? Can you give an example of a time in your life when you have experienced what you might call a 'living hope'? [Tracks 32-3 on the CD/transcript.]

9. **Read Romans 8.18-27.** Has a suffering person ever asked you deep questions about a living hope? Or have you perhaps been the person in pain asking the questions? Share experiences within your group.

10. **Read 1 Peter 1.6-7** and the box at the top of p. 18. 'As Christians, the reason we can rejoice is because we know that "now" is not all there is' (p. 19). Does your faith help you when you go through tough times and/or as you consider your own mortality? How sure are you about what awaits you when you die – do you have a 'living hope'? [Tracks 32-3 on the CD/transcript.]

11. **Read 1 John 3.2-3** and the box from the Book of Common Prayer on p. 17. How can 'hope' be 'sure and certain'? What do you think the Christian word 'hope' means? How is this different from the way we use the word in everyday conversation?

Looking ahead, you may wish to bring a Bible to the next session – and perhaps a candle (and matches!)

SESSION 5

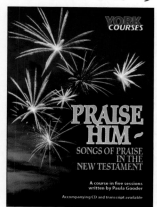

WORD MADE FLESH

Word Made Flesh: John 1.1-14

No reflection on the great poetic sections of the New Testament would be complete without John 1. It seems right to end with arguably the greatest piece of poetic theology in the Bible. John 1.1-14 is sublime. It is regularly read aloud at Christmas and I find it hard not to be caught up in the beauty of the words. It is a passage to be savoured and enjoyed simply for its sound and feel; it is also a passage to be reflected on. As with the other passages we've looked at in this course, we are spoilt for choice, but have to choose just a few of the themes on offer.

The opening part of John 1 has very similar themes to Colossians 1.15-20 (Session 2). Key themes in both are:

- Christ being with God in creation
- Christ being the agent of creation

John's Gospel, however, takes these themes one step further. Verses 1-3 are connected to verse 10: John tells us that because the world came into being through Jesus, the world should have recognized him.

Awesome wonder

I'm not alone in loving the hymn *O Lord my God, when I in awesome wonder consider all the works thy hand hath made*. As with all great hymns the tune is very good, but it's the words that grab you. What the hymn-writer tells us in the first two verses is that there are places in the world that simply make him want to praise God.

I know exactly what he means. Some places make my soul yearn to sing *'how great thou art'*. In those places I do find it easier to recognize God for the great Creator that he is; and by extension to recognize Christ for his role in creation too.

John 1 takes this one step further (as does Paul in Romans 1). John appears to think that because the world came into being through Christ, we human beings *ought* to have been able to recognize him. In other words, there is a deep connection between the world and Jesus Christ, and this deep connection should give us the ability to know Christ when we encounter him. At the same time, John recognizes that this is not the case. The world did not, and does not, recognize the one through whom everything came into being.

21

Light and dark

Woven around this is a related theme which John loves: light and darkness. Anyone who has ever lit a candle or a lamp outside in summer knows all too well that within moments a whole host of insects, particularly moths, are drawn to the light. What is less obvious is that other insects are repelled by it – cockroaches scurry away from the light as fast as they can.

The theme John's Gospel plays with here is that of the attractiveness or otherwise of light. The problem with light is that it shines on everything. You can't edit it so that it shines on some things and not on others. The implication of the language John uses is that some people preferred darkness: they did not want the light that Jesus brought to shine too brightly on them.

Another element of John's image is the battle that takes place between light and darkness. This is referred to in verse 5: *'The light shines in the darkness, and the darkness did not overcome it.'* In our modern electrically lit world this concept is hard to understand; but light a candle in a dark room and the notion is much easier to grasp.

Electric light banishes darkness almost immediately. First it is dark and then it is light. But with a candle it can appear as though the light is pushing the darkness back. As the flame strengthens and grows, so the darkness recedes around it. The light of Jesus came to push back the darkness – slowly but irrevocably. No wonder those who liked the dark neither welcomed nor accepted him.

John may be playing on words in verse 5 as well. Those familiar with John 1 in the King James Version (as many are from Christmas services) will know that the KJV translates verse 5 as *'And the light shineth in darkness; and the darkness comprehended it not.'* This seems to suggest that the issue was not so much about victory, as about understanding. The Greek word John uses here (*katalambanō*) can be translated either as

- 'overtake' or 'overcome' (i.e. victory) or
- 'find out about' or 'understand' (i.e. comprehend)

The connection is that you can overtake things with your mind and hence have victory over them.

When *katalambanō* is used elsewhere in John it has the meaning of 'seized' or 'taken' (John 8.3-4). So most modern translations have opted for that meaning here.

But this whole passage is about recognition and knowing 'the Word'. I wonder if John used a word with two meanings here deliberately – the darkness couldn't *overcome* the light of Christ and – at the same time – did not *understand* it either.

Mixing metaphors

One of the features I most enjoy about the New Testament authors is that they haven't been to the English lesson that tells them not to mix their metaphors. Both John and Paul appear to take the greatest delight in mixing metaphors. In John 1 Jesus is both 'the word' and 'the light' (although these two don't quite go together).

In verse 14 a third metaphor is introduced, although it's harder to see this in the English translation. John 1.14 can be translated as *'and the Word became flesh and pitched his tent among us'.* You can see why translators opt for the more obvious *'lived among us'.*

Yet we miss something with this translation. Something both formal and informal is suggested by 'pitched his tent among us'. It takes us all the way back to the book of Exodus and God's 'tabernacle' – which was a tent. It reminds us that when God first dwelt among his people, he did so in a tent.

At the same time it also suggests something gloriously *informal*: Jesus came and set up camp among us. In other words, he mucked in and became just like us, so that he could help us out of the darkness to live in the light that he brought.

*

Over this course we've looked at some immense and mind-blowing ideas of the greatness, the wonder and the awe that God and Jesus Christ evoke. But it seems right to end with this ordinary image. An ordinary image that is at the same time the most wonderful of all: God loved the world so much that he sent his Son to pitch his tent among us; to live like us; to be one of us – and by doing so, to point us to God and bring us salvation.

QUESTIONS FOR GROUPS
BIBLE READING: John 1.1-14

1. Spend a few quiet moments reflecting on **John 1.1-14**. Which phrases 'speak' to you most clearly? Why do you think people love this passage so much?

2. **Read Psalm 139.8.** 'Then sings my soul, my saviour God to thee'. Is there a particular place where you find yourself closest to God? Or can you sense the presence of God anywhere/everywhere?

3. **Read John 1.6-9.** When John describes Jesus as the 'light of the world' what do you think he meant? In what ways do you think Jesus 'enlightens' (a) the world and (b) us? Can you share with your group a time when Jesus has brought light into your life?

4. **Read John 8.12** and the box at the top of p. 22. John explores the attractiveness of Jesus, light of the world. Why do you think that some people were attracted to him and others fled from or opposed him?

5. **Read Matthew 5.14-16.** In the Sermon on the Mount Jesus tells his rag-tag followers, *'You are the light of the world.'* What might this mean for us today?

6. On track 34 the Archbishop remembers Christians at school who were given a hard time because of their faith. Have you experienced hostility/mockery for your beliefs? How might we encourage young people in their faith?

7. **Read John 1.14** and read the box with Irenaeus' words on p. 21. Have you seen or sensed the glory of God? If so, when? And what was it like?

8. **Read John 1.17.** John tells us that Jesus was/is 'full of grace and truth'. What do you understand by this? On track 38 Archbishop Justin speaks of people with these qualities who've inspired him. Have you met people who've inspired you by showing Jesus' qualities of grace and truth in their own lives?

9. Is there a topic arising from this course which you would like to raise or revisit?

10. Look ahead. What is the future for your group? Meet again? Another course – or disband? Perhaps hold a social event (a coffee morning maybe) and invite others to join you?

11. Re-read the final para of Session 5 (below the asterisk). It is a thumbnail summary of the Christian faith. Spend a few moments quietly reflecting on these words. You might wish to close with Moira Sleight's suggestion [CD track 41] to light a candle, dim the other lights and ask a group member to read John 1.1-14 aloud.

When I look back on my Hebridean childhood, some of the most wonderful people I've known were devout (Calvinist) Presbyterians. People like the late Katie Maclennan of Seaforth Head who, when I asked her in 2011, 'Do you not get lonely, do you not get afraid, living all alone, the last person in the village by the light of your oil lamp?' responded, 'How can I be lonely, how can I be afraid, when I'm with God?'

Alastair McIntosh, writer and academic

Which leading Christians would you like to hear at your next discussion group?

YORK COURSES

have an extensive list of ecumenical courses, suitable for any time of year – including Lent and Advent. All are ideal for discussion groups, and individual reflection. The majority of our courseshave 5 sessions, but there are 4- and 6-session courses too, and the range is growing every year. There's something for everyone! All of the following have a course booklet with questions, plus an accompanying CD and transcript.

4-SESSION COURSE
IDEAL FOR ADVENT–OR ANY SEASON

JESUS: the voice that makes us turn

Course booklet written by Bishop David Wilbourne

Reflecting on Jesus' many voices. *A Crying Voice* homes in on the baby's cry at Bethlehem; *An Other Voice* focuses on the strangeness of Christ, whose command stilled the storm and forgave sins and raised the dead. *A Dying Voice* sees new depths for living in Jesus' familiar words from the cross. *A Rising Voice* examines the immense quality which made downhearted disciples turn and fire the world with their faith. Four different voices that will make us turn in our tracks and say to Christ, 'I want you!'

Bishop David Wilbourne in relaxed conversation with Canon Simon Stanley, with contributions from churchgoers of different denominations.

5-SESSION COURSES - SUIT▢

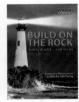

BUILD ON THE ROCK
Faith, doubt – and Jesus

Is it wrong – or is it normal and healthy – for a Christian to have doubts? Is there any evidence for a God who loves us? We hear from many witnesses. At the heart of a Christian answer stands Jesus himself. We consider his 'strange and beautiful story' and reflect upon his teaching, his death, his resurrection and his continuing significance.

With Bishop Richard Chartres, Dr Paula Gooder, Revd Joel Edwards and Revd David Gamble.

GLIMPSES OF GOD
Hope for today's world
Course booklet written by Canon David Winter

We live in turbulent times. This course draws on the Bible, showing where we can find strength and encouragement as we live through the 21st century.

With Rt Hon Shirley Williams, Bishop Stephen Cottrell, Revd Professor David Wilkinson and Revd Lucy Winkett.

HANDING ON THE TORCH
Sacred words for a secular world

Worldwide Christianity continues to grow at an immense pace. At the same time in the West it struggles to grow and – perhaps – even to survive. But what might this mean for individual Christians, churches and Western culture, in a world where alternative beliefs are increasingly on offer?

With Archbishop Sentamu, Clifford Longley, Rachel Lampard and Bishop Graham Cray.

RICH INHERITANCE
Jesus' legacy of love
Course booklet written by Bishop Stephen Cottrell

Jesus left no written instructions. By most worldly estimates his ministry was a failure. Nevertheless, Jesus' message of reconciliation with God lives on. With this good news his disciples changed the world. What else did Jesus leave behind – what is his 'legacy of love'?

With Archbishop Vincent Nichols, Paula Gooder, Jim Wallis and Inderjit Bhogal.

WHEN I SURVEY...
Christ's cross and ours
Course booklet written by Revd Dr John Pridmore

The death of Christ is a dominant and dramatic theme in the New Testament. The death of Jesus is not the end of a track – it's the gateway into life.

With General Sir Richard Dannatt, John Bell, Christina Baxter and Colin Morris.

These three...
FAITH, HOPE & LOVE

Based on the three great qualities celebrated in 1 Corinthians 13. This famous passage begins and ends in majestic prose. But the middle paragraph is practical and demanding. St Paul's thirteen verses take us to the heart of what it means to be a Christian.

With Bp Tom Wright, Anne Atkins, the Abbot of Worth and Professor Frances Young.

THE LORD'S PRAYER
praying it, meaning it, living it

In the Lord's Prayer Jesus gives us a pattern for living as his disciples. It also raises vital questions for today's world in which 'daily bread' is uncertain for billions and a refusal to 'forgive those who trespass against us' escalates violence.

With Canon Margaret Sentamu, Bishop Kenneth Stevenson, Dr David Wilkinson and Dr Elaine Storkey.

CAN WE BUILD A BETTER WORLD?

We live in a divided world and with a burning question. As modern Christians can we – together with others of good will – build a better world? Important material for important issues.

With Archbishop John Sentamu, Wendy Craig, Leslie Griffiths and five Poor Clares from BBC TV's 'The Convent'.

LE FOR ANY TIME OF YEAR

WHERE IS GOD...?

To find honest answers to these big questions we need to undertake some serious and open thinking. Where better to do this than with trusted friends in a study group around this course?

With Archbishop Rowan Williams, Patricia Routledge CBE, Joel Edwards and Dr Pauline Webb.

BETTER TOGETHER?

Course booklet written by Revd David Gamble

All about relationships – in the church and within family and society. ***Better Together?*** looks at how the Christian perspective may differ from that of society at large.

With the Abbot of Ampleforth, John Bell, Nicky Gumbel and Jane Williams.

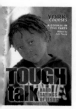

TOUGH TALK
Hard Sayings of Jesus

Looks at many of the hard sayings of Jesus in the Bible and faces them squarely. His uncomfortable words need to be faced if we are to allow the full impact of the gospel on our lives.

With Bishop Tom Wright, Steve Chalke, Fr Gerard Hughes SJ and Professor Frances Young.

NEW WORLD, OLD FAITH

How does Christian faith continue to shed light on a range of issues in our changing world, including change itself? This course helps us make sense of our faith in God in today's world.

With Archbishop Rowan Williams, David Coffey, Joel Edwards, John Polkinghorne and Dr Pauline Webb.

IN THE WILDERNESS

Like Jesus, we all have wilderness experiences. What are we to make of these challenges? ***In the Wilderness*** explores these issues for our world, for the church, and at a personal level.

With Cardinal Cormac Murphy-O'Connor, Archbishop David Hope, Revd Dr Rob Frost, Roy Jenkins and Dr Elaine Storkey.

FAITH IN THE FIRE

When things are going well our faith may remain untroubled, but what if doubt or disaster strike? Those who struggle with faith will find they are not alone.

With Archbishop David Hope, Rabbi Lionel Blue, Steve Chalke, Revd Dr Leslie Griffiths, Ann Widdecombe MP and Lord George Carey.

JESUS REDISCOVERED

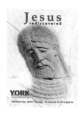

Re-discovering who Jesus was, what he taught, and what that means for his followers today. Some believers share what Jesus means to them.

With Paul Boateng MP, Dr Lavinia Byrne, Joel Edwards, Bishop Tom Wright and Archbishop David Hope.

4-SESSION COURSE
EXPECTING CHRIST

Looking at several moments in our faith and lives where a door opens and lets Christ in, catching the sense of expectancy which not only comes at the season of Advent, but throughout the year.

FOUR SESSIONS: Expecting Christ in family; Expecting Christ in me; Expecting Christ in prayer; Expecting Christ in the end.

Bishop David Wilbourne and Canon Simon Stanley in relaxed conversation, with contributions from a variety of churchgoers.

"... the excellent series of York Courses designed for groups and individuals."
Church Times review

TWO 6-SESSION COURSES

LIVE YOUR FAITH

Christianity isn't just about what we believe: it's about how we live. A course suitable for everyone; particularly good for enquirers and those in the early stages of their faith.

With Revd Dr Donald English, Lord Tonypandy, Fiona & Roy Castle and Baron John Habgood.

GREAT EVENTS, DEEP MEANINGS

Explains clearly what the feasts and fasts are about and challenges us to respond spiritually and practically. There are even a couple of quizzes to get stuck into!

With Revd Dr John Polkinghorne KBE FRS, Gordon Wilson, Bishop David Konstant, Fiona Castle, Dame Cicely Saunders, Archbishop David Hope.

York Courses also have books, booklets – and CD Conversations featuring leading Christian thinkers. A selection of these is shown below to whet your appetite. Please visit www.yorkcourses.co.uk where detailed information on the full range is available. You can listen to sound bites from the CDs, and view sample pages from our course booklets and transcripts, as well as order online.

CD CONVERSATIONS

Hawking, Dawkins and GOD

John Polkinghorne KBE FRS, distinguished scientist and Anglican Priest, discusses his Christian faith in the light of the New Atheism.

CD	**£5**
Transcript (emailed as a PDF)	**£2.60**
Paper transcript (sent by post)	**£3.10**

Rowan Revealed
The 104th Archbishop of Canterbury talks about his life and faith, prayer, the press, politics, the future of the Church...

CD	**£3.50**
Transcript booklet	**£3.10**

Climate Change and Christian Faith
Nobel Prize winner Sir John Houghton CBE, FRS, a world expert on global warming, on why he believes in Climate Change and in Jesus Christ. **£5**

Science and Christian Faith
An in-depth discussion with the Revd Dr John Polkinghorne KBE FRS, former Cambridge Professor of Mathematical Physics **£5**

Prayer **£3.50**
Four Christians on praying... for healing; in danger; in tongues; with perseverance. This CD accompanies the booklet *The Archbishop's School of Prayer.*

Multipacks of CDs available at www.yorkcourses.co.uk

PAPERBACKS
by CANON JOHN YOUNG

Special prices for paperbacks by John Young

Lord... Help my unbelief **£8.50**
"John Young is an outstanding communicator of the Christian message" *(Canon David Winter)*

Christianity – an introduction **£7.99**
"An exciting, engaging and intellectually serious book" *(Archbishop Rowan Williams)*

Christianity made simple **£4.99**
A short and to-the-point guide to Christianity, set out in just 96 pages.

These prices are valid until 1 June 2015. Please contact our office for a current copy of our full list of courses and publications, including prices.

T: **01904 466516** / E: **courses@yorkcourses.co.uk**
Or download a copy from **www.yorkcourses.co.uk**